IF... MARCHES ON

Steve Bell

for Heather

Also by Steve Bell
Apes of Wrath
Unspeakable If...
Unstoppable If...
Bell's Eye: Twenty Years of Drawing Blood
If... Bottoms Out
The If... Files

Steve Bell and Brian Homer
Chairman Blair's Little Red Book

FIDELIS ULTRA TAMPAX

The Five Tests

Gordon Brown's restatement of the five tests that needed to be passed before Britain could join the single European currency seemed to contradict the Prime Minister's apparent enthusiasm for the project.

9.6.03

9

Roadmap To A Noo Yurp

President Bush impressed the Polish leadership with his knowledge of European history when he announced that 'Russia is not the enemy. Russia is – you know . . . the idea of Russian tanks storming across Europe are no longer the problem.'

16.6.03

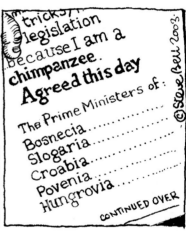

11

Can You Walk Backwards?

The government's proposal to abolish the position of Lord Chancellor was blocked by the House of Lords. Meanwhile a self-styled 'Comedy Terrorist' dressed as Osama bin Laden gatecrashed Prince William's 21st birthday inside Windsor Castle.

23.6.03

13

Is The Pope Catholic?

Foreign Secretary Jack Straw's diplomatic storytelling abilities have often been remarked upon, but never his uncanny resemblance to the Demon Headmaster.

30.6.03

15

Illegal Combatants

As the War on Terror hotted up in the wake of the coalition's achievements in Iraq, the population of illegal combatants detained at Guantanamo in Cuba got bigger.

7.7.03

Summer Holiday With Cliff

The Prime Minister needed to spend some much-needed recovery time at his friend Sir Cliff Richard's holiday home in Barbados.

14.7.03

19

Intelligence Failure

The suicide on July 17th of Dr David Kelly, former UN weapons inspector in Iraq and intelligence expert at the Ministry of Defence, cast severe doubts over the intelligence that had been used to justify the invasion of Iraq.

18.8.03

23

Imagine I'm Lord Hutton

The Prime Minister's chief spin doctor, Alastair Campbell, came under suspicion of misrepresenting intelligence in order to justify the war. An inquiry into the circumstances surrounding Dr Kelly's death was set up under Lord Hutton. Defence Minister Geoff Hoon seemed doomed.

25.8.03

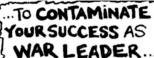

Alastair – Don't Go!

Alastair Campbell resigned preemptively, but the Prime Minister was still under intense pressure as a result of the Hutton Inquiry's investigations.

1.9.03

27

Bring It On!

President Bush asked Congress for $87,000,000,000,000 dollars to fund the war and reconstruction in Iraq. Congress found it difficult to object to such an obvious bargain.

6.9.03

29

Because He's Worth It

Speculation as to the whereabouts of the Mickey Mouse of global terrorism, Osama bin Laden, was still rife, but not as rife as it might have been.

15.9.03

31

Flatlining Those Blues Away

Having been the only major party to oppose the war, the Liberal Democrats hoped to increase their support in the country. Leader Charles Kennedy seemed relaxed.

22.9.03

A Future Fair For All

After the bruising divisions over the war in Iraq, Tony Blair felt it was time for him to reconnect with the membership at the Labour party conference in Bournemouth.

29.9.03

'Wo bee to you that are full, for yee shall hunger. And by the Prophet Esaias hee cryeth out, Wo be to you that rise vp early to giue your selues to drunkennes, & set all your mindes so on drinking, that you sit swilling thereat vntill it bee night.'

From 'Certaine Sermons Or Homilies appointed to be read in Churches, In the time of the late Queene Elizabeth of famous memory' (London, 1623)

A Fair Deal For Everyone

The Conservative party conference in Blackpool posed enormous questions for Iain Duncan Smith, whose leadership was proving marginally less charismatic than a glass of water.

6.10.03

The High-Pitched Screaming Of A Quiet Man

Despite the seventeen standing ovations he had received for his closing conference speech, Iain Duncan Smith's position as party leader seemed increasingly insecure.

13.10.03

41

Tired, Listless, Twitchy

The Prime Minister received emergency electro-cardiac treatment to regulate heart palpitations, a condition known as 'supraventricular tachycardia'.

20.10.03

The Butler Goes Free

After being cleared of stealing certain personal items belonging to the late Princess Diana, her former butler and 'rock' Paul Burrell sold his story exclusively to the *Mirror* and found himself under fire from every single other newspaper.

27.10.03

The Quiet Man Dissolves

Iain Duncan Smith finally stepped down as leader of the Tory party, giving way to former Home Secretary Michael Howard, who was elected unopposed.

3.11.03

47

Don't Mention The Butler

There was much speculation in the tabloids concerning relations between Prince Charles and certain trusted servants.

10.11.03

50

'The quiet man is here to stay and he's turning up the volume.'

Iain Duncan Smith, in his closing speech to the party conference in Blackpool, Thursday October 9th 2003.

George Bush Comes To Town

The Queen played host to the President and his wife at Buckingham Palace during his visit to London. The Bushes flew back home via Teesside airport, paying a social call to Tony Blair in his Sedgefield constituency in County Durham.

17.11.03

Thanksgiving

In the wake of the President's visit, thoughts turned to the absence of a British public holiday at this time of the year. The former Labour rebel Ken Livingstone, now successful Mayor of London, was allowed back into the Labour party.

24.11.03

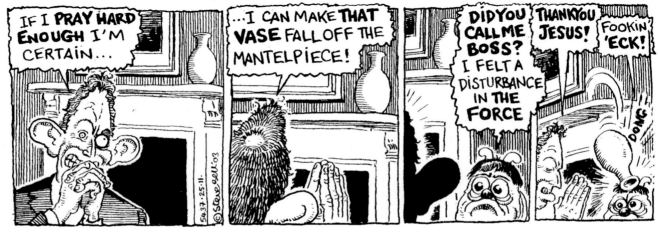

Conversation With Britain

In order to reconnect with the British people, the Prime Minister launched his Big Conversation on the topics they really cared about.

1.12.03

57

Iraq Gets The Bird

President George Bush flew secretly to Iraq to present a turkey to the troops there. The actual turkey he was photographed with was in fact made of plastic.

8.12.03

59

Xmas In X-Ray

Saddam Hussein was captured as he hid in a small hole near his home town of Tikrit in central Iraq.

15.12.03

Inner Turmoil

Beset by questions raised by the Hutton Inquiry, Prime Minister Blair sought reassurance by visiting British troops in Iraq.

5.1.04

63

Mission To Mars

In a visionary speech President Bush spoke of his intention to get a man to Mars.

12.1.04

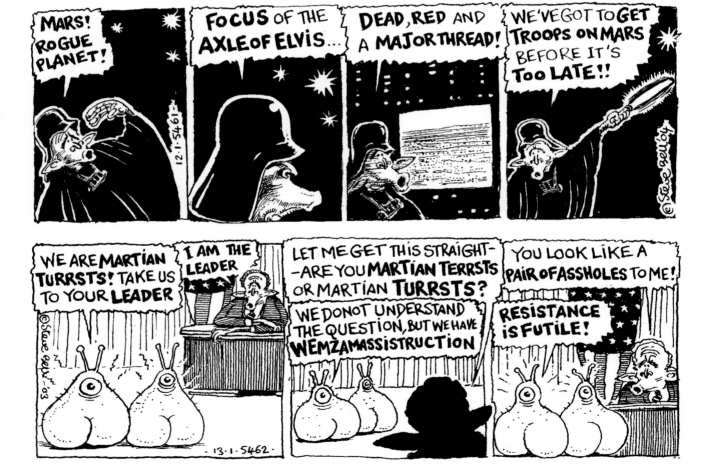

65

Lest ye corrupt yourselves, and make you a graven image, the similitude of any figure, the likeness of male or female,

The likeness of any beast that is on the earth, the likeness of any winged fowl that flieth in the air,

The likeness of any thing that creepeth on the ground, the likeness of any fish that is in the waters beneath the earth.

Deuteronomy 4: 16–18

Then Paul stood in the midst of Mars' hill, and said, Ye men of Athens, I perceive that in all things ye are too superstitious.

Acts 17: 22

Newness Renewed

Britain's bid for the 2012 Olympics depended on the renewal of Britain's world-class transport infrastructure.

19.1.04

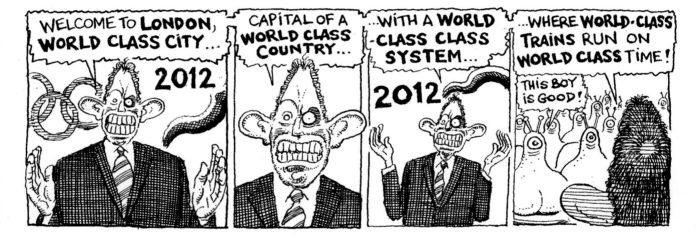

The White Stuff

The report by Lord Hutton into the events surrounding the suicide of weapons expert Dr David Kelly cleared the Prime Minister of any taint of wrongdoing. The BBC on the other hand was made an example of, and the Director-General Greg Dyke, the Chairman Gavyn Davies and the journalist Andrew Gilligan all resigned.

2.2.04

Blue Skies

Faced with an unexpected slump in popularity in the wake of his exoneration by the Hutton report, the Prime Minister needed the kind of fresh thinking that only Lord Birt, the former Director-General of the BBC, was capable of.

11.2.04

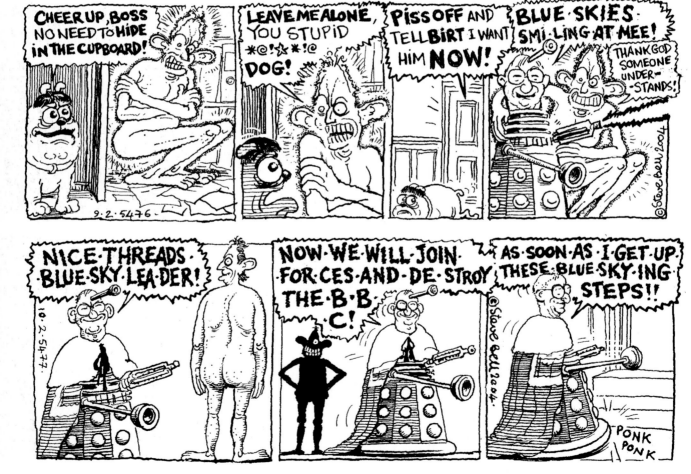

Benefit Tourists

A number of British citizens who had been held without charge for as much as two years in Guantanamo's Camp X-Ray were returned to Britain where, after being detained in police custody for a few days, they were released without charge.

23.2.04

The British People Want To Move On

While acknowledging that his intelligence on weapons of mass destruction in Iraq had been flawed, the Prime Minister insisted that the invasion had been carried out in good faith.

8.3.04

A Fistful Of Euros

Chancellor Gordon Brown, outlining his eighth Budget to the Commons, ruled out a further assessment of the five economic tests for Britain's joining the euro. He also announced massive civil service job cuts.

15.3.04

79

And if ye shall despise my statutes, or if your soul abhor my judgments, so that ye will not do all my commandments, but that ye break my covenant:

I also will do this unto you; I will even appoint over you terror, consumption, and the burning ague, that shall consume the eyes, and cause sorrow of heart: and ye shall sow your seed in vain, for your enemies shall eat it.

And I will set my face against you, and ye shall be slain before your enemies: they that hate you shall reign over you; and ye shall flee when none pursueth you.

Leviticus 26: 15–17

Am I Dead Yet?

Though it had been over two years since the greatest manhunt in history had begun, Osama bin Laden was still at large. Known to be in need of kidney dialysis, there were reports that he was dying and in need of medical attention.

22.3.04

Blame It On The Bogey

To demonstrate consistent opposition to evil dictatorships, Prime Minister Tony Blair met the reformed despot Colonel Gaddafi in a tent in the Libyan desert. Gaddafi showed him the soles of his feet.

29.3.04

TONY – I HAD TO CALL TO **THANK YOU** FOR YOUR WORK...

LET ME TELL YA THIS FROM THE **BOTTOM** OF MY HEART:

YOU'RE NO POODLE, PRIMESTER **TONY BLAIR**...

YOU'RE MY SPECIAL **BOGEYMAN BARGEPOLE!!**

INTENSE PRIDE

31·3·5503

– Steve Bell 2004 –

WHILE YOU'RE **ON THE LINE**, TONY...

...I HEAR YER HAVIN' TROUBLE WITH **XYLOPHONE SEEKERS**...

I KNOW YOU'LL **APPRECIATE MY ADVICE** ON THIS ONE, PRIMESTER:

I MAJORED IN GOOD **VIBES AT YALE** SO I KNOW WHAT I'M TALKIN' ABOUT...

1·4·5504

©Steve Bell '04

SHALL WE **PRAY TOGETHER**, PRIMESTER TONY?

ARE YOU **KNEELING** COMFORTABLY? THEN I'LL **BEGIN**...

LORD: SPARE US FROM **XYLOPHONE** SEEKERS WITH **EVELYN TENT**...

...AND MAY **ALL** OUR BOGEYMEN BE **FRENZA FREEDOM!!**

12·4·5505

©Steve Bell 2004

Archbishops' Wives

A hard-hitting series on the terrible pressures afflicting the home lives of our top clerics.

5.4.04

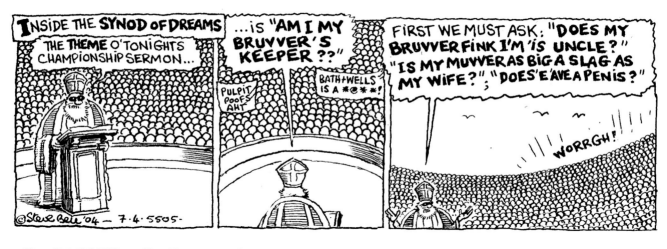

Where Is The Roadmap?

When asked about his relationship with the President, the Prime Minister replied that they stood shoulder to shoulder. When asked in relation to the war on Iraq whether he would have done anything differently, the President was lost for words.

19.4.04

How Much A Gallon?

Rising oil prices signalled a shift of priorities for the President. The Saudi Prince Bandar bin Sultan had long been a personal friend to the Bush family.

26.4.04

91

The John Reid Health Plan

Health Secretary John Reid was concerned about the Prime Minister's general state of health. It was time for him to use his head.

3.5.04

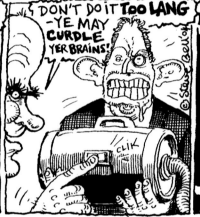

A Dog's Life

The confident pride in their work felt by members of the American occupying force was faithfully recorded in a famous series of photographs.

10.5.04

95

And then shall appear the sign of the Son of man in heaven: and then shall all the tribes of the earth mourn, and they shall see the Son of man coming in the clouds of heaven with power and great glory.

And he shall send his angels with a great sound of a trumpet, and they shall gather together his elect from the four winds, from one end of heaven to the other.

Matthew 24: 30–32

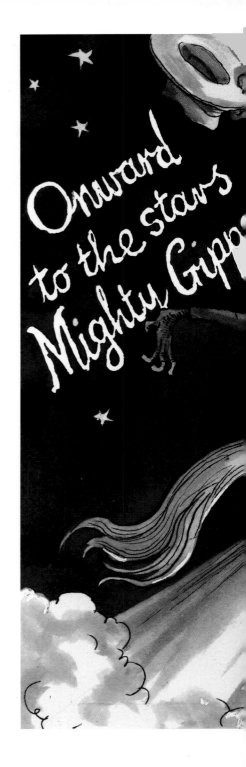

The Truth About The Arabs

Driven out of his long running daytime chat show by political correctness gone mad at the BBC for simply telling the truth in his newspaper column, Robert Kilroy-Silk joined the UK Independence Party.

17.5.04

Free Ahmed Chalabi!

Former Iraqi exile and favourite of the US administration, Ahmed Chalabi had fallen out of favour with the American authorities in Iraq, led by Paul Bremer. In the run-up to the handover of sovereignty to the interim Iraqi government, Chalabi distanced himself from his former paymasters and moved close to the Shiites.

24.5.04

Saving Bush's Privates

President Bush visited Normandy for the sixtieth anniversary of D-Day. Meanwhile former President Ronald Reagan led an assault on heaven.

7.6.04

103

Significant Numbers

As the end of the occupation approached, an accurate cost-benefit analysis of the war in Iraq would show that, in return for a comparatively modest outlay, there had been substantial gains in civilian mortality and unprecedented reductions in the number of poor people there.

13.6.04

105

The Book Tour

Former President Bill Clinton went on tour to promote his autobiography.

21.6.04

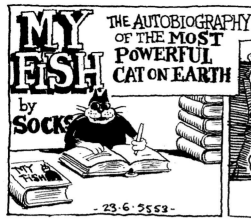

Camp X-Box

In the aftermath of the Hutton report the BBC felt honour bound to get on the right side of government, so a BBC College of Journalism was proposed.

28.6.04

If you want to find the old battalion,
I know where they are, I know where they are.
If you want to find the old battalion,
I know where they are,
They're hanging on the old barbed wire.
I've seen 'em, I've seen 'em,
Hanging on the old barbed wire,
I've seen 'em, I've seen 'em,
Hanging on the old barbed wire.

Traditional First World War song

Gordy No Balls

Ed Balls, Gordon Brown's closest advisor at the Treasury, went off to pursue a political career as the Labour candidate for the safe constituency of Normanton in Yorkshire.

5.7.04

The Butler Report

The Review of Intelligence on Weapons of Mass Destruction led by former Cabinet Secretary Lord Butler of Brockwell was finally published. Some detected the faintest note of criticism in its pages.

12.7.04

The Dream Ticket

As the US presidential election approached there were questions asked about the Vice President's state of health.

18.7.04

Reshuffle Fever

Summer's heat brought on sudden outbreaks of reshuffle fever at the highest levels of government. The knives were out and blood would flow. Except it didn't.

26.7.04

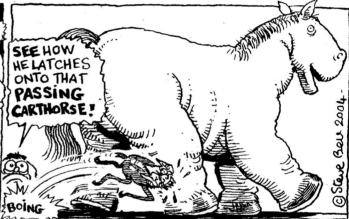

119

Meet The People

George Bush's election campaign gathered momentum as the US death toll in Iraq passed 1,000.

6.9.04

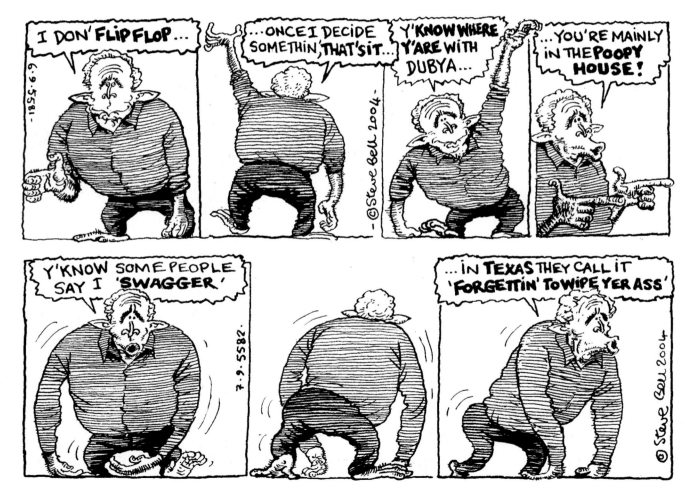

121

Dogging With Foxes

The Commons voted once again to outlaw hunting with dogs. This time however the Parliament Act was invoked to by-pass the House of Lords which meant that it would actually become law in due course. Alan Milburn was appointed to run Labour's election campaign. Gordon Brown was not happy.

13.9.04

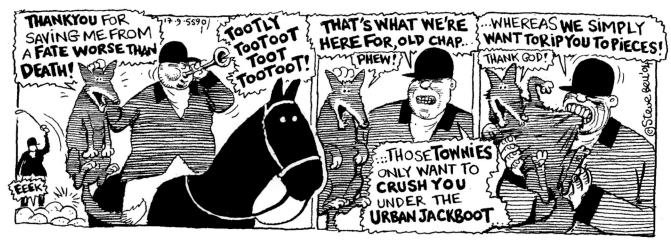

123

Wednesday September 15th 2004:

At 4.20pm five protesters burst into the Commons chamber as members debated the ban on hunting with dogs, causing the temporary suspension of parliamentary business.

Four of the men appeared from behind the Speaker's chair on the opposition side while another tried to wrestle past the doorkeeper at the other end of the chamber. One of them shouted, 'This isn't democracy. You are overturning democracy!' at Rural Affairs Minister Alun Michael. A scuffle ensued during which several of the protesters were overturned.

After the resumption of business, MPs voted to back a ban by 339 to 155 votes.

32·16·9·04-

125

Chuckence Of Libralia

With courage and determination, Charles Kennedy faced the prospect of five days without a drink in the sweltering hell of the Bournemouth party conference.

20.9.04

127

A Better Life For All

Pro-hunting demonstrators eager to show their concern at the future of the countryside almost disrupted the Labour conference in Brighton by distributing a dead horse and some dead dogs around the city centre. A good point was well made. Alan Milburn made no impression at all and George Bush stayed at home.

27.9.04

129

Surge To Power

In Bournemouth the Conservatives held their first conference with Michael Howard as leader. Shadow Defence Minister Nicholas Soames had expressed concern at their lack of progress in the polls.

4.10.04

131

A Secret Republican

The race for the presidency entered the final stretch. Questions were raised as to which candidate the Prime Minister would prefer to win, but no answers were given. In a televised debate with John Kerry, a faltering George Bush was seen to have a suspicious lump on his back, under his jacket.

11.10.04

133

The American People Decide

The Presidential election took place on Tuesday November 2nd. George Bush appeared to win a second term.

1.11.04

135

Darling, I'm Home

After George Bush's re-election Tony Blair made sure he was the first foreign dignitary to pay him a visit.

8.11.04

137

'I earned capital in the campaign, political capital, and now I intend to spend it. It is my style. That's what happened in the . . . after the 2000 election, I earned some capital. I've earned capital in this election . . . and I'm going to spend it for what I told the people I'd spend it on, which is . . . you've heard the agenda: Social Security and tax reform, moving this economy forward, education, fighting and winning the war on terror.'

George Bush,
White House press conference,
November 4th 2004.

© Steve Bell 2004 — AFTER CHARLES ADDAMS —

~2153· 3.11.04 ~

Blue Skies Full Of Outside The Box Bats

Michael Howard had honed the Tory message down to eleven words: School Discipline, More Police, Cleaner Hospitals, Lower Taxes, Controlled Immigration, and Accountability.

15.11.04

141

Santa's Pre-Budget Report

Gordon Brown shrugged off economic worries in his pre-election pre-budget report. After revelations concerning the fast-tracking of his former girlfriend's nanny's application for a work permit, David Blunkett resigned as Home Secretary.

6.12.04

Voting For Christmas

As the death toll among US troops in Iraq rose inexorably, so did complaints about conditions there. Secretary of Defense Donald Rumsfeld remained unmoved.

13.12.04

145

Feed The Hungry

In the aftermath of the tsunami, and in the midst of starvation and Aids in Africa and elsewhere, altruism was back on the agenda. So too were the tensions between Tony Blair and Gordon Brown, hungry as ever to succeed.

10.1.05

147

Inauguration Day

George Bush's second inauguration ceremony took place without incident, unlike the first where he had been chased by an angry mob.

17.1.05

149

The Da Blairi Code

A member of Tony Blair's cabinet belonged to the Roman Catholic sect 'Opus Dei', whose members were reputed to wear the cilice, a kind of spiky garter worn to mortify the flesh.

24.1.05

151

Take up the White Man's burden –
Send forth the best ye breed –
Go, bind your sons to exile
To serve your captives' need;
To wait, in heavy harness,
On fluttered folk and wild –
Your new-caught, sullen peoples,
Half devil and half child.

Take up the White Man's burden –
In patience to abide,
To veil the threat of terror
And check the show of pride;
By open speech and simple,
An hundred times made plain,
To seek another's profit
And work another's gain.

Take up the White Man's burden –
The savage wars of peace –
Fill full the mouth of Famine,
And bid the sickness cease;
And when your goal is nearest
The end for others sought,
Watch Sloth and heathen Folly
Bring all your hope to nought.

Take up the White Man's burden –
Ye dare not stoop to less
Nor call too loud on Freedom
To cloak your weariness;
By all ye will or whisper,
By all ye leave or do,
The silent sullen peoples
Shall weigh your gods and you.   Rudyard Kipling

...and Bush create

emocracy

©Steve Bell 2005 - AFTER MICHELANGELO

153

Housey Housey

As anti-terror proposals piloted by Home Secretary Charles Clarke became more draconian and there were further reports of the abuse of prisoners held by the British in Iraq, Tony Blair said: 'The difference between democracy and tyranny is not that in a democracy bad things don't happen, but that when they do happen people are held and brought to account. That is what is happening under our judicial system.'

31.1.05

155

Out Of The Frying Pan

As the government talked up its anti-terror proposals for internment of suspects without trial, so too it emphasised the probability of 'death and destruction on an unlimited scale'.

7.2.05

157

Forward Not Back

As a counter to Michael Howard's eleven words, Labour came up with several more: Your Family Better Off, Your Family Treated Better And Faster, Your Child Achieving More, Your Country's Borders Protected, Your Community Safer, Your Children With The Best Start, topped off with the slogan 'Britain Forward Not Back'.

14.2.05

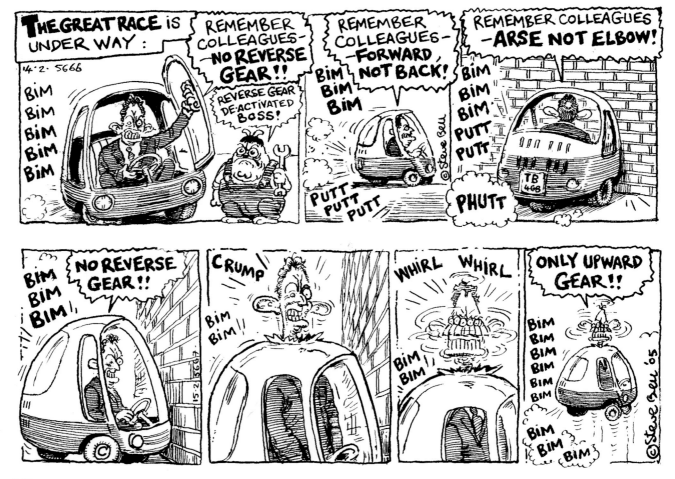

A Noo Yurp

A New Europe was taking shape in President George Bush's imagination as he embarked on a whirlwind sequence of meetings with European leaders, ending up at a summit in Bratislava, Slovakia, with Russian President Vladimir Putin.

21.2.05

161

Celebrity Surgeon's Academy

Unusually for a Conservative leader, Michael Howard went on the offensive in an election campaign on the subject of the National Health Service, citing one woman's experience of failing to get the operation she required, in support of his proposals for a 'Patient's Passport'.

7.3.05

Bat-Beating Brow Jabs

The Prime Minister's brow seemed suspiciously unfurrowed as he faced an unexpected assault from the Cardinal Archbishop of Westminster, Cormac Murphy O'Connor, after Michael Howard expressed a personal preference for reducing the time limit on abortions.

14.3.05

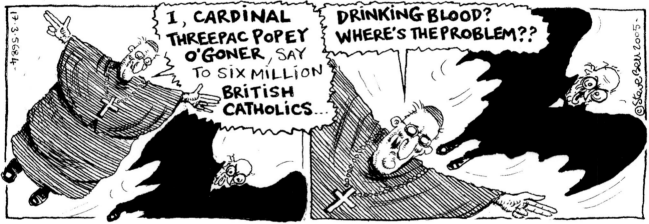

165

*'There is a crack packet – crack packet o' fame,
She hails from Noo York, an' the Dreadnought's her name.
You may talk o' your fliers – Swallow-tail and Black Ball –
But the Dreadnought's the packet that can beat them all.'*

Rudyard Kipling, Captains Courageous

Vote Vampire

In order to command greater respect and credibility, Michael Howard employed Australian political hit-man Lynton Crosby to take charge of the Conservative campaign.

21.3.05

They're Off!

Parliament was dissolved, the politicians went to the country, the Pope died and the Prince of Wales had to delay his wedding to Camilla Parker Bowles by one day to avoid a clash with the funeral.

4.4.05

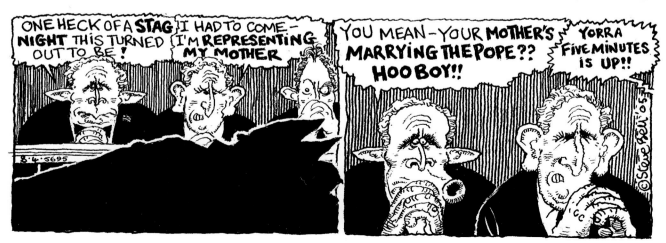

171

Manifesto Fever

The poster campaigns hotted up, the manifestos were launched and Liberal Democrat leader Charles Kennedy became a father for the first time.

11.4.05

173

The Prince of Wales had to abandon his original plans to marry in Windsor Castle after discovering that the licence permitting a civil ceremony there would run for three years. This would have enabled commoners to marry in the castle, which is the Queen's favourite residence, so the venue was switched to Windsor's Guildhall at very short notice.

All Beads And Biscuits

The Cardinals assembled in the Sistine Chapel in Rome to find a successor to John Paul II. Cardinal Ratzinger was elected to become Pope Benedict XVI.

18.4.05

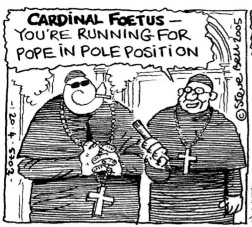

CARDINAL FOETUS — YOU'RE RUNNING FOR POPE IN POLE POSITION

WHAT WOULD YOU SAY TO **WOMEN PRIESTS?**

I SAY: **TONIGHT YOU SLEEP WID DA FISHES!**

THANKS TO ANDREW SANNHOLM

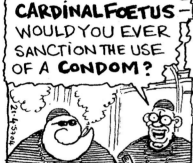

CARDINAL FOETUS — WOULD YOU EVER SANCTION THE USE OF A **CONDOM?**

NOPE! ISSA **NEVER EVER** JUSTIFIED, **NO WAY, NO CHANCE,** NOT EVEN WID A **CHOIR BOY...**

NOT EVER, AT ALL, PERIOD.

EXCEPT MAYBE WHEN YOU **ROBBIN' A BANK!**

SKRAWK

SKREEK

THANKS TO ANDREW SANNHOLM

I AM THE POPE! I AM THE POPE!! EVERYBODY KNOWS THAT I AM THE POPE!

POPEHEIL!! POPEHEIL!!

HOLY FATHER — **WHAT** ARE YOU GOING TO **CALL YOURSELF?** ARE YOU GOING TO REMOVE YOUR **SUN- GLASSES?**

BELIEVER'S VOICE

I'M TAKING THE NAME STRANGELOVE XXX!!

Time Bombs And Holes Of Colour

The Tories struggled to move an increasingly bad-tempered campaign onto the heavily coded issues of race, asylum and immigration.

25.4.05

United Front

As the campaign reached its climax, Gordon Brown and Tony Blair were seen to be uncomfortably inseparable. A curiously relaxed Blair had clearly been putting on weight.

2.5.05

181

Humble People

Having conceded defeat despite having increased the number of Conservative seats, Michael Howard expressed his intention to stand down as party leader later in the year.

9.5.05

183

Going Through the Motions ~

MILLAIS ~

After the election was over, in a rally in the newly Conservative seat of Putney, Michael Howard announced:

'I'm 63 years old. At the time of the next election in four or five years' time I'll be 67 or 68, and I believe that's simply too old to lead a party into government. So, as I can't fight the next election as leader of our party I believe its better for me to stand aside sooner rather than later, so that the party can choose someone who can.'

Tony Blair had already expressed his intention to stand down after serving a full third term.

The Respect Agenda

The newly re-elected Prime Minister vowed to address the issues of antisocial behaviour and offensive clothing.

16.5.05

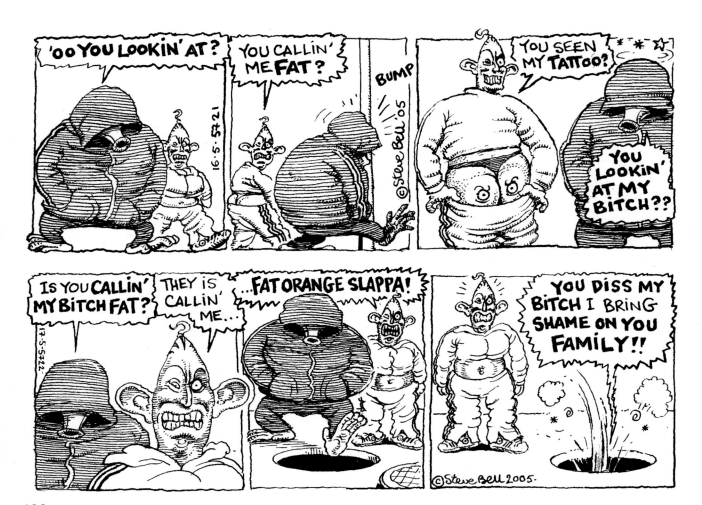

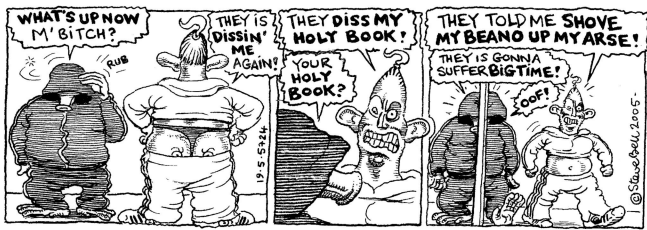

187

Oui Ou Non?

The French held a referendum on the proposed European Constitution as drafted by former President Giscard d'Estaing. It was decisively rejected by the French, and the Dutch electorate did the same shortly afterwards.

23.5.05

Panel 1: MA LURVELY LEEDLE CRAPAUD SAY: A "OUI" VOTE... / OUI! OUI! OUI!

Panel 2: ...WILL ENSURE PEACE AND PROS-PERITÉ WHILE PRESERVING ZE BEST OF WHAT IS FRANCH...

Panel 3: ...LIKE, PAR EXAMPLE, 'IS LEGS!

Panel 4: A "NON" VOTE MEANS THE TOAD WILL DIE!!

Panel 5: THE COQ'E SAY A "NON" VOTE... / NONNANONNANON!

Panel 6: ...WILL KEEP ZE FEELTHY ROSBIFS FROM ATTACKINGUE...

Panel 7: ...ZE FULL FRANCH LURNCH WITH WAHN!!

Panel 8: SAY "NON" TO ZE STINKINGUE SANDWICH AT ZE DESK!! / SPRRLLT

Panel 9: IF YOU 'ATE* ZE ROSBIFS VOTEZ "OUI!" VOTEZ "OUI!" / IF YOU REALLY 'ATE ZE ROSBIFS VOTEZ "NON!" VOTEZ "NON!"

Panel 10: "OUI" WILL PROTECT YOU FROM SAVAGE ROSBIF-STYLE FREE MARKET! / SAY "NON" TO ENFORCED ROSBIF-STYLE FREE MARKET SAVAGERY!

Panel 11: OUI NON NON OUI NONNONNON OUI OUI OUI OUI NON NON NON OUI OUI OUI !!!

*TO THE TUNE OF 'IL Y A UN 24-HEURE TAVERNE DANS LE TOWN

189

Live 8

Veteran rock star and poverty campaigner Bob Geldof proposed a giant demonstration in Edinburgh and a concert in Hyde Park on the theme of global trade justice, to coincide with the G8 summit of world leaders at Gleneagles in July. He also proposed a Dunkirk-style flotilla of sailing boats to go over to France and bring back supporters from the continent. Surprisingly, the latter idea failed to raise interest.

6.6.05

191

Africa Corp®

Millions sent texts to secure their free Live 8 concert tickets. Some questioned the absence of African artists on the bill of a show devoted to Africa, and an alternative venue was proposed for such acts at the Eden Project down in Cornwall.

13.6.05

193

Harmful Emissions

After giving President Bush such staunch support over security issues, Prime Minister Blair had hoped for reciprocal back-up when he sought to take a lead on the need to tackle global warming.

20.6.05

195

The Single European Cows

Mankind stood at the crossroads. In order to avert global catastrophe, an historic choice needed to be made between ruminant quadrupeds and royalty.

27.6.05

197

G8 Breakthrough

The long-awaited G8 summit of leaders from the world's most powerful economies took place at Gleneagles in Scotland. President Bush gave a wide-ranging and exclusive interview to ITN's veteran newscaster, Sir Trevor Macdonald.

4.7.05

DULCE ET DECORUM EST PRO PATRIA MORI

© Steve Bell 2005-

OVER THE TOP

When you're wounded and left on Afghanistan's plains,
And the women come out to cut up what remains,
Jest roll to your rifle and blow out your brains
An' go to your Gawd like a soldier.

Rudyard Kipling, The Young British Soldier

Aftershock

Four home-grown suicide bombers struck the London Transport Underground just as the G8 summit was coming to an end. Over fifty people were killed and hundreds were injured. Prime Minister Blair was swift to unite the country by denying any idea that this might be some form of retaliation for Britain's presence in Iraq.

11.7.05

203

Inflammatory Language

It was proposed that describing suicide bombers as 'martyrs' should be outlawed in the forthcoming anti-terror bill.

18.7.05

Reaching Out To The Muslim Community

The Royal Institute for International Affairs issued a report which stated that 'Riding pillion with a powerful ally has proved costly in terms of British and American lives . . . and the damage caused to the counter-terrorism campaign'.

25.7.05

Goat Gourmet

British Airways had subcontracted the manufacture and supply of pre-cooked meals for all its flights to a company named Gate Gourmet, which unilaterally attempted to impose new working conditions on its largely Asian workforce. A wildcat strike ensued that caused massive disruption to BA flights at the height of the holiday season.

29.8.05

Hurricane Katrina

Large tracts of the Gulf coast were devastated by Hurricane Katrina. President Bush's inadequate response to the disaster was attributed by some to the fact that most of those worst affected, particularly in the low-lying flooded areas of the city of New Orleans, were both poor and black. Thousands appeared to have been abandoned in the Superdome stadium without power, food or water.

5.9.05

Ich Bin Ein Berliner

In the great debate between tabloid and broadsheet, the *Guardian* finally opted for an historic compromise by adopting the 'Berliner' format, which is like a tabloid but a bit deeper (i.e. longer top to bottom, but not much wider). Produced at brand-new printing works, it became the first British newspaper to be printed in colour on every page. Though reluctant at first, the *If...* strip eventually took to it like a penguin to a jacuzzi.

12.9.05

POLICE? THERE'S A MAD, DRUGGED-UP PENGUIN RUNNING RIOT!

- 14·9·5783 -

...PLUS SOMEBODY'S NICKED DOONESBURY!

...AND NOW MY BEAK'S TURNED ORANGE! COME QUICK!!

© Steve Bell '05

NAH THEN, NAH THEN! WHAT'S-A-GOIN' ON 'ERE??

AAARRGH! THE BOY'S IN BLUE!

BASE TO BADGER: WHAT'S-A-GOIN' ON THERE THEN?

GO AWAY!

BADGER TO BASE: IT'S COLOUREDS 'AVIN' A DOMESTIC! I'M LEAVIN' IT ALONE!!

ORANGE BEAK!!

YELLOW FEET!! NO!

GREAT TAN, TONY!

16·9·5785

© Steve Bell '5

I GOT SOMETHIN' TO SHOW YOU TOO. I BEEN WORKIN' ON IT ALL SUMMER!

MY PURPLE ASS!

The torn boughs trailing o'er the tusks aslant,
The saplings reeling in the path he trod,
Declare his might – our lord the Elephant,
Chief of the ways of God.

The black bulk heaving where the oxen pant,
The bowed head toiling where the guns careen,
Declare our might – our slave the Elephant,
And servant of the Queen.

Rudyard Kipling, Beast & Man in India

Cross-Party Consensus

Home Secretary Charles Clarke was involved in cross-party talks with his opposite numbers David Davis of the Conservatives and Mark Oaten of the Liberal Democrats in drafting his anti-terror bill.

19.9.05

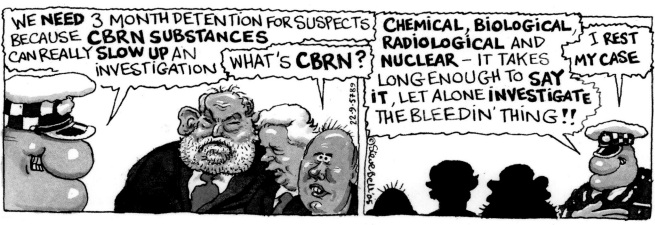

217

I'm A Celebrity – Who The Fuck Am I?

The Conservative party conference in Blackpool was a kind of beauty parade for the five candidates for the leadership: Dr Liam Fox, Sir Malcolm Rifkind, David Cameron, David Davis and Kenneth Clarke.

3.10.05

I'M A CELEBRITY - WHO THE FK AM I?**

I'M SO **FRESH** AND **MODERN** MY FACE ACTUALLY **HURTS**.

BUT POLITICS IS ABOUT **MORE** THAN MY **FAT FACE** AND MY **SMALL MOUTH**...

...IT'S ALSO ABOUT MY **ENORMOUS SPOON!**

I'M A CELEBRITY - WHO THE FK AM I?**

I'M THE ONLY CANDIDATE THAT'S **TRAINED TO KILL**...

...WITH HIS **BARE HANDS!**

AUTO THROTTLE

I'M A CELEBRITY - WHO THE FK AM I?**

THERE'S ONLY **ONE THING** TO REMEMBER ABOUT ME...

IT'S NOTHING TO DO WITH **FAGS, HATS, PAUNCHES** OR **HUSH PUPPIES**...

...IT'S THE FACT THAT I'M A **ONE WASTELAND CONSERVATIVE!**

219

With God On His Side

The world reeled when President Bush sensationally stated that God had told him to invade Afghanistan and Iraq.

10.10.05

GEORGE—REMEMBER WHEN I TOLD YOU TO **INVADE AFGHANISTAN?**

I REMEMBER IT, LORD, **CLEAR AS DAY!!**

12·10·5998·

HOW DID YOU KNOW IT WAS **ME** TALKING?

NOONE ELSE SPEAKS TO ME OUT OF A **PINK** CLOUD, LORD!

PINK IS FOR HOMOS, GEORGE! **PURPLE** IS THE **LORD'S COLOUR**

I'LL GET MY **EYES TESTED** RIGHT AWAY, LORD!

©Steve Bell 2005

GEORGE—WHY WOULD I TELL YOU TO **INVADE AFGHANISTAN?**

·13·10·5799·

YOU SAID IT WAS TO BRING **FREEMAN MOXY** TO THE **TOWELHEADS**, LORD!

THAT'S **LIBERAL FAGGOT** TALK— —I DON'T '**DO**' DEMOCRACY

©Steve Bell 05

I'M MORE OF AN '**OBEY ME OR I SMITE**' KIND OF GUY

GOT SOME **TABLETS OF STONE** HERE FOR YOU, GEORGE

CLUNK

YOW LORD!

·14·10·5800·

...JUST SO THERE'S **NO CONFUSION**

THANK YOU LORD!

1: NO GAY WEDDINGS
2: SMITE THE ABORTIONISTS
3: TAX BREAKS FOR THE RICH

4: INVADE ANY TOWELHEAD COUNTRY YOU LIKE
5: ER.... THAT'S IT!

©Steve Bell 2005·

WOW! WAIT TILL I TELL **DICK!**

SUCKER!

1: NO GAY WEDDINGS
2: SMITE THE ABORTIONISTS
3: TAX BREAKS FOR THE RICH

4: INVADE ANY TOWELHEAD COUNTRY YOU LIKE
5: ER.... THAT'S IT!

Return Of The Blunkett

After his earlier resignation from the post of Home Secretary, David Blunkett was briefly rehabilitated as Minister for Work and Pensions.

17.10.05

223

Strictly For The Birds

The threatened pandemic caused by a newly mutated bird flu virus appeared to be getting closer.

24.10.05

Penguins Going Straight

The popular French documentary *March of the Penguins*, about the life history of the Emperor penguin, was interpreted by the religious right in the USA as confirmation of its most deeply held beliefs.

31.10.05

227

The Camel's hump is an ugly lump
Which well you may see at the Zoo;
But uglier yet is the hump we get
From having too little to do.

Rudyard Kipling, Just So Stories

The Pants Of Power

A new book by Sir Christopher Meyer, the ex-Ambassador to Washington at the time of the invasion of Iraq, criticised the Prime Minister's craven attitude to his American ally, as well as his taste for ball-crushingly tight trousers.

14.11.05

Straight Bishops

The Church of England was still riven over the issues of women priests and gay clergy. A reactionary vicar who attempted to perform ordinations with a like-minded bishop imported from outside his own diocese was reprimanded and stripped of his licence.

21.11.05

233

No Fish, No Sex, No Daylight

Long-range forecasts were predicting one of the coldest winters for years. Or not.

28.11.05

235

I'm A Nonentity – Get Me In There!

The Conservative leadership elections reached their climax when the result of the final membership ballot was announced. David Cameron beat David Davis by 134,446 votes to 64,398. William Hague returned to frontline politics as Cameron's Shadow Foreign Secretary.

5.12.05

Extraordinary Rendition

The CIA practice of seizing terrorist suspects and transferring them to countries which are less circumspect in their attitude to the use of torture came briefly under the spotlight.

12.12.05

Ming, Destroyer Of Worlds

Charles Kennedy's leadership of the Liberal Democrats was undermined by widespread gossip about his addiction to alcohol. The Windsors retreated to Sandringham.

19.12.05

Wild Boar Ahoy!

Animal rights protesters released a large group of wild boar from a farm. The local hunt, short of legal things to do since the anti-hunting legislation had finally come into force, offered its services to recapture the beasts, without much success.

9.1.06

'. . . the White House is called the people's house, and we're going to call Marshmallow and Yam the people's turkeys. They made it here through a democratic process. There was a nationwide election on the White House website. In the end, the voters made the choice, and it was a close election. You might say it was neck and neck.'

George Bush, November 22nd 2005

© Steve Bell 2005 - 23

Grace And Favour Doghouse

There were questions as to whether the deputy Labour leader John Prescott had paid the correct amount of council tax on his London residence. He also expressed doubts over aspects of the Prime Minister's latest batch of education reforms.

16.1.06

Whale Meat Again

A disoriented young twenty-foot-long female bottlenosed whale strayed up the Thames into central London. A rescue attempt was made but the whale died (of hunger and thirst, it transpired after the autopsy).

23.1.06

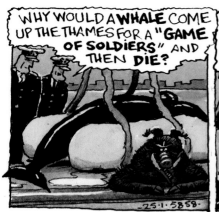

249

Operation Wee Jobbie

Defence Secretary John Reid announced plans to send an increased force of up to 3,500 British troops to the most lawless and dangerous parts of southern Afghanistan. In the same week, the death toll of British servicemen in Iraq rose to one hundred.

30.1.06

Drawing God

The publication of a number of cartoons of the prophet Mohammed in the Danish newspaper *Jyllands-Posten* caused widespread outrage across the Muslim world.

6.2.06

And he that beareth the carcase of them shall wash his clothes, and be unclean until the even: they are unclean unto you.

These also shall be unclean unto you among the creeping things that creep upon the earth; the weasel, and the mouse, and the tortoise after his kind,

And the ferret, and the chameleon, and the lizard, and the snail, and the mole.

Leviticus 11: 28–30

Spot The Difference

There are ten key points of difference between these two drawings.
The artist cannot remember what they are. Can you find them?